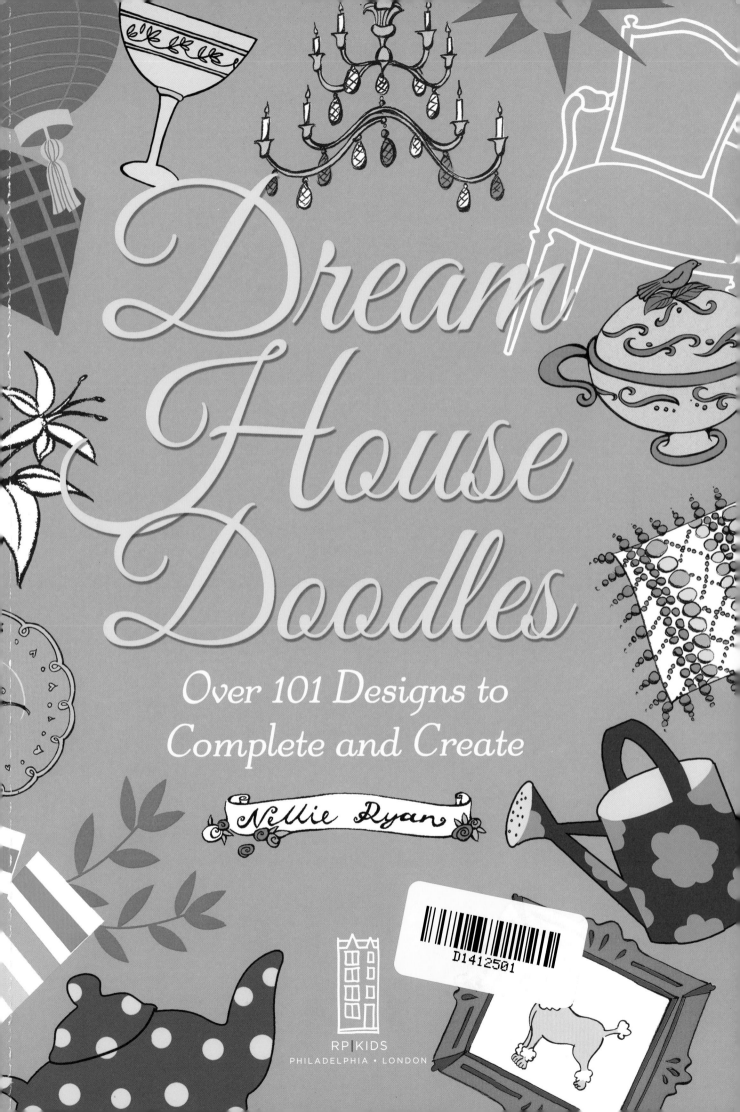

Dream House Doodles

Over 101 Designs to Complete and Create

Nellie Ryan

RP|KIDS
PHILADELPHIA • LONDON

First published in Great Britain in 2008 by Buster Books,
an imprint of Michael O'Mara Books Limited, 9 Lion Yard, Tremadoc Road, London SW4 7NQ.

First published in the United States by Running Press Book Publishers, 2008

Printed in China

Books published by Running Press are available at special discounts for bulk purchases in the United States
by corporations, institutions, and other organizations. For more information, please contact the
Special Markets Department at the Perseus Books Group, 2300 Chestnut Street, Suite 200, Philadelphia,
PA 19103, or call (800) 810-4145, ext. 5000, or e-mail special.markets@perseusbooks.com.

ISBN 978-0-7624-5292-7

9 8 7 6 5 4 3 2 1
Digit on the right indicates the number of this printing

Illustrated by Nellie Ryan
Edited by Sally Pilkington
Cover by Zoe Quayle

This edition published by:
Running Press Kids
An Imprint of Running Press Book Publishers
A Member of the Perseus Books Group
2300 Chestnut Street
Philadelphia, PA 19103–4371

Visit us on the web!
www.runningpress.com/kids

WELCOME!

This book offers you the chance to let your creativity shine, as you become a real-life interior designer. You'll be able to transform drab decor into desirable design, and express your own unique style and flair.

There are sections in this book that encourage you to design everything a dream home could need, from lavish living rooms and bold bedrooms, to beautiful bathrooms and cutting-edge kitchens. Then head outdoors to create a glorious garden.

There's an Interior Design Studio section where, like a true professional, you can decorate your own workspace, design a window display for your shop, and create a catalog to show off your cool design collection.

Don't hang around watching the paint dry! Grab your pen and start doodling inspiring interiors.

Sally

Editor

The Living Room Collection

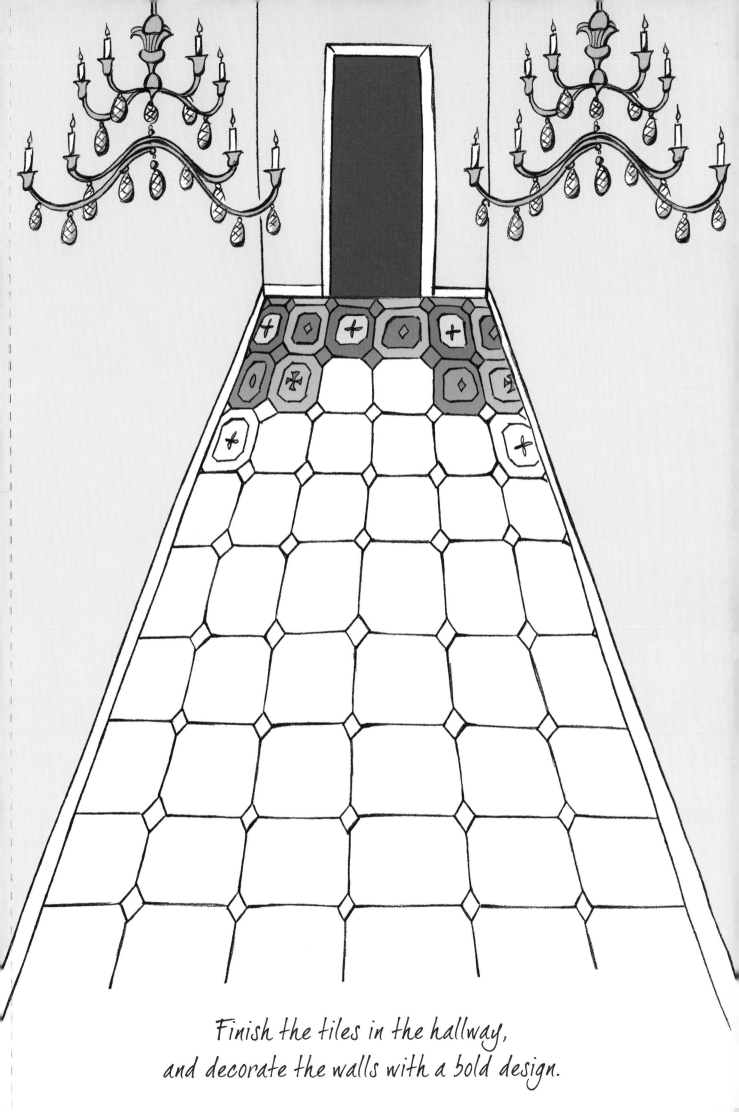

Finish the tiles in the hallway,
and decorate the walls with a bold design.

Home is where the hearth is.

Warm your heart and your home with a traditional fireplace.

Wipe your feet!

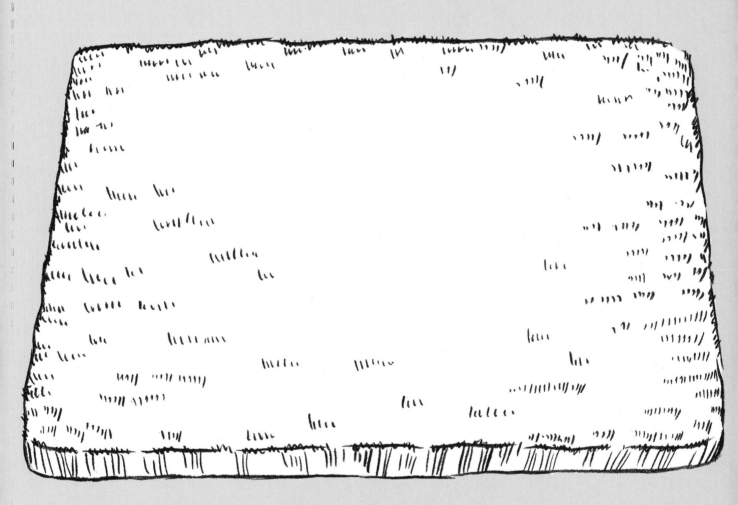

Create a welcoming design for the doormat.

In with the old.

Design a striped fabric,
then cover the chair with it.

Give antique furniture a fresh look with some serious stripes.

Picture perfection.

Create a masterpiece to go above the fireplace.

Time to put your feet up.

Bold footstools are a stylish way to take the weight off your feet.

Give them bright patterns to make them stand out.

Sofa so good.

Cover the sofa with supersoft cushions in pretty patterns.

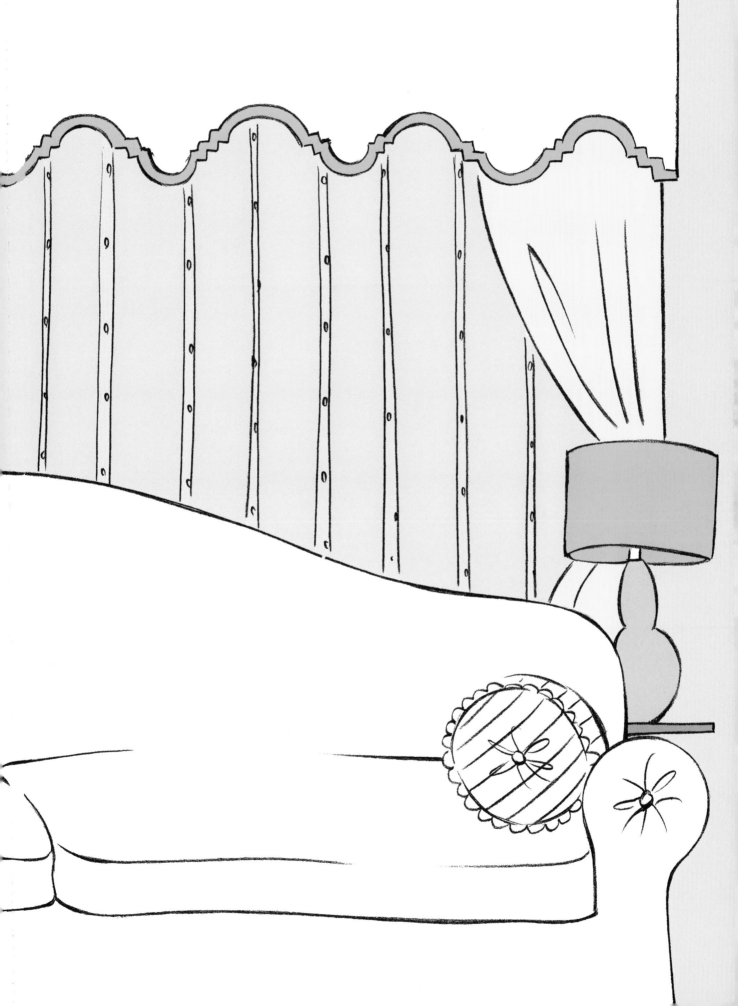

On the shelf.

Fill the shelves with more gorgeous ginger jars.

Shelves don't have to be boring!
Fill these zigzag shelves with plants and knickknacks.

Comfortably chic.

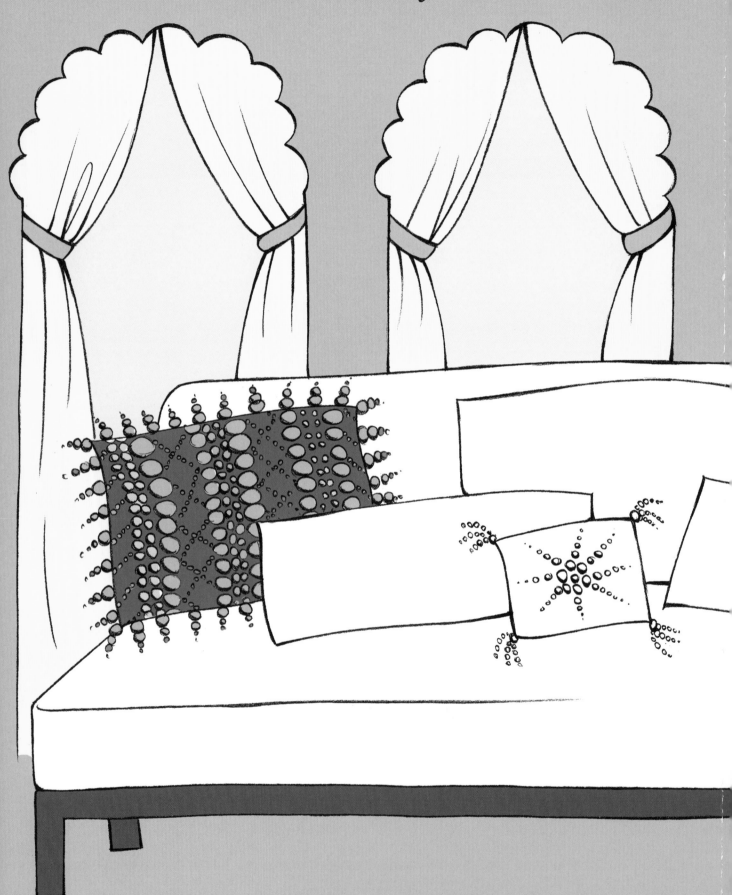

Crystals and sequins add a luxurious look to your room.

Glamorize your cushions with sparkly crystals and sequins.

Magic carpets.

An exotic carpet can really warm up
your room and your feet.

Finish this bold carpet's daring design.

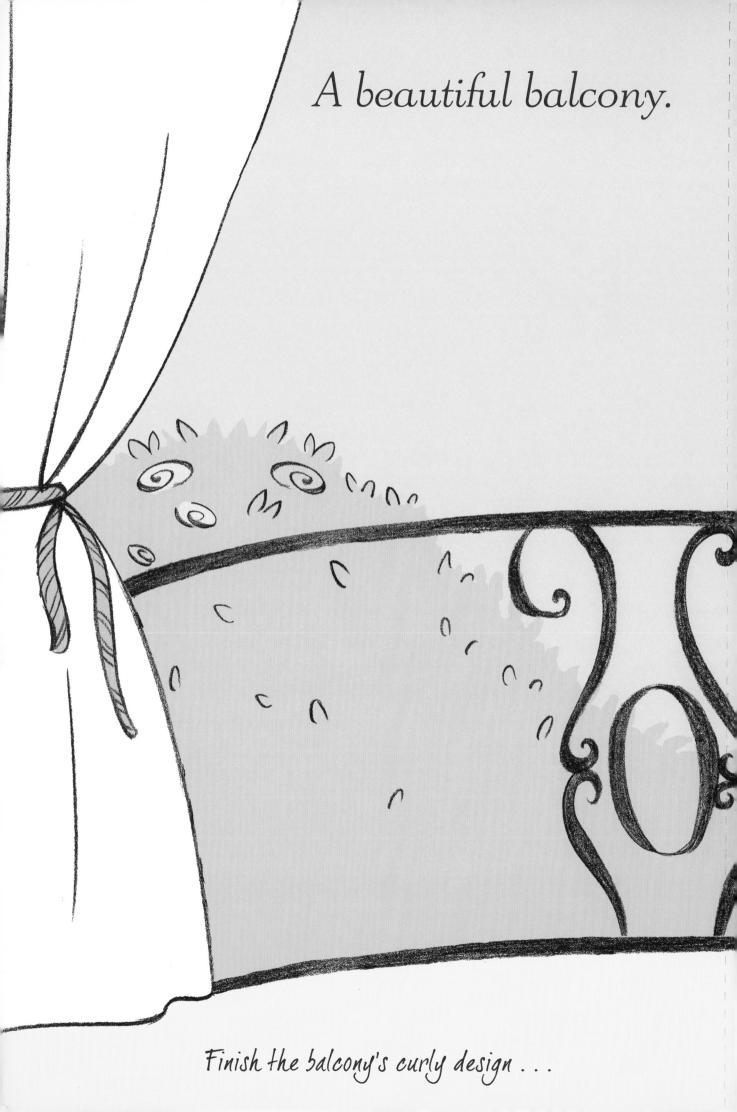

A beautiful balcony.

Finish the balcony's curly design . . .

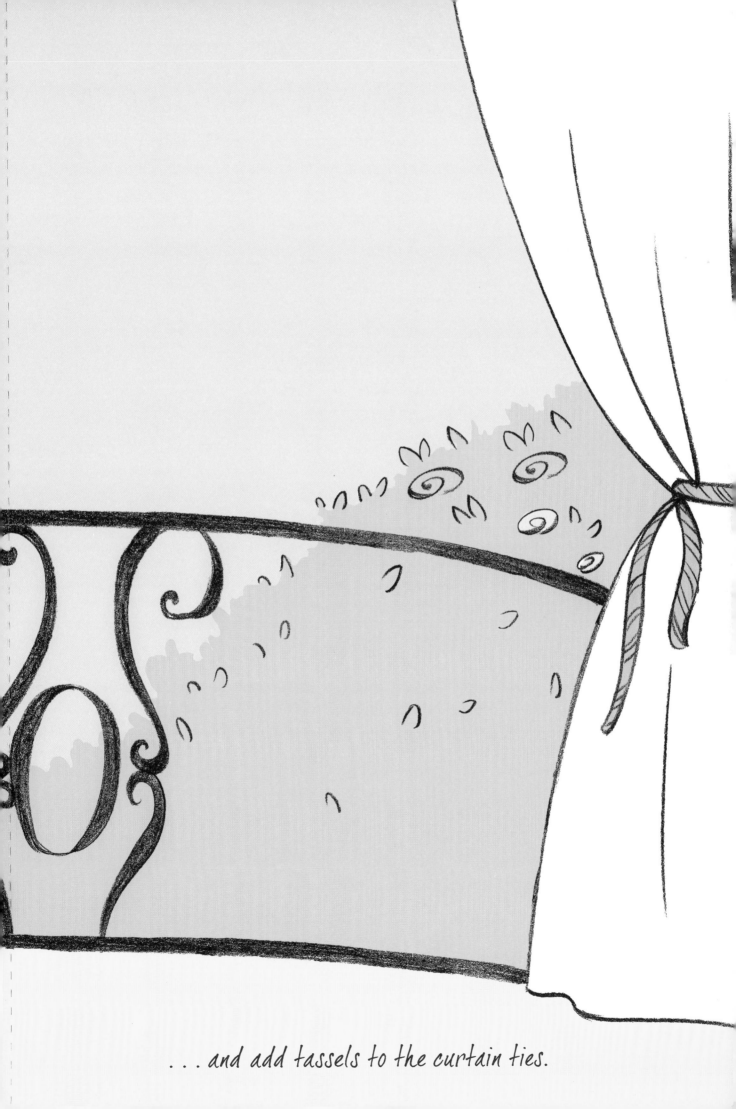

. . . and add tassels to the curtain ties.

Flower power.

Value your vases. Fill them with fabulous floral displays.

Give this beautiful bouquet a vibrant vase.

Out with the old . . .

Tired, dull furniture can be given
a new lease on life with pretty, patterned patches.

. . . in with the new look.

Revamp this old sofa with
a cozy mixture of fabric patches.

Cane couture.

Natural cane can give your room a tropical vibe.
Finish this fabulous cane chair.

Oh, so opulent!

Finish the Chinese carpet's intricate design.

A room with a view.

Draw a gorgeous view and finish the comfy spot to admire it from.

The Bathroom Collection

Laid-back luxury.

Finish the marvelous mural on the bathroom wall.

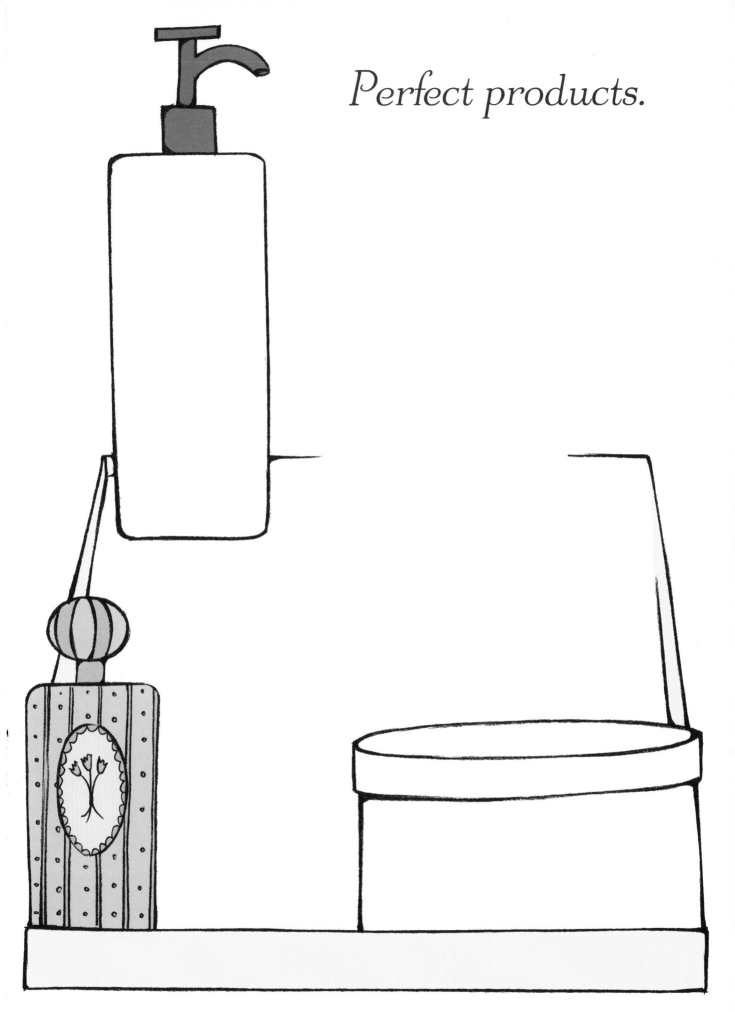

Perfect products.

Design your own range of beautifully packaged
bathroom products.

Bathroom for improvement.

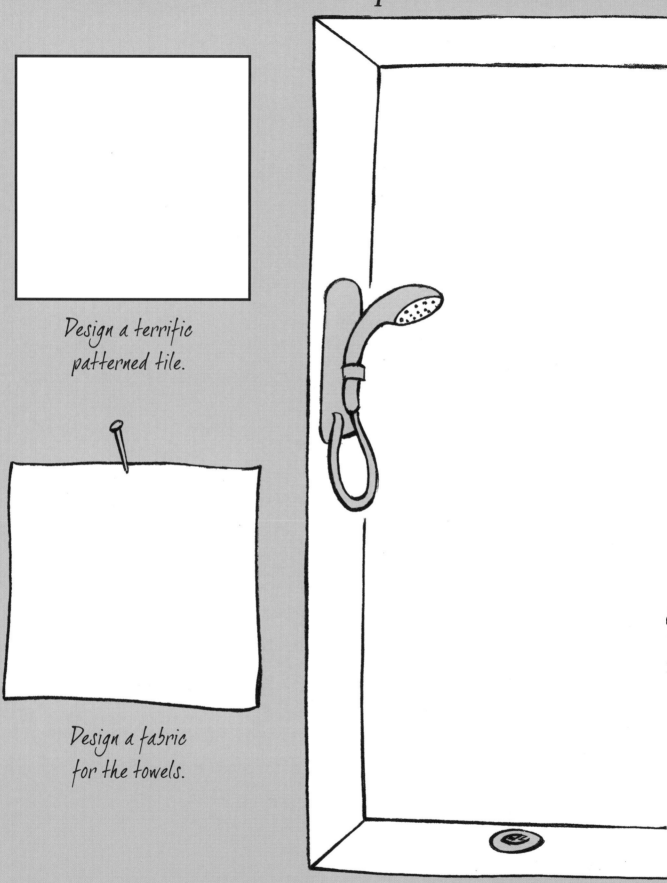

Design a terrific
patterned tile.

Design a fabric
for the towels.

Make a splash in the bathroom by covering
the walls with your tiles.

Make washed-out bathrooms a thing of the past.
Give the mirror a bold frame.

Pull the plug on dull taps.

Design some vintage taps.

Fit your taps to this sink.

Design some
modern taps.

Fit your taps to this sink.

Curtain call.

Finish this ducky design.

Finish this bubbly design.

Make a splash with a beautiful showstopping shower curtain.

Cover the curtain in a design of your choice.

Bargain beach chic.

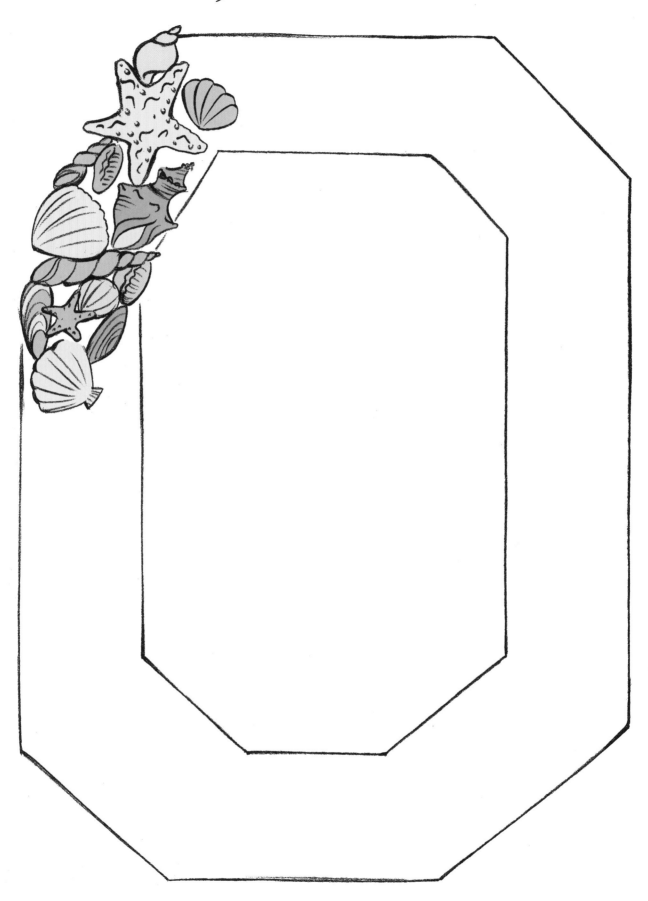

Cover the mirror with seaside finds for instant vacation glamour.

Go girly!

Fill the dainty dish with pretty-shaped soap.

The ocean floor.

Finish the mosaic for a beautiful bathroom floor.

What's your tile style?

Design a gorgeous range of tiles.

Terrific towels.

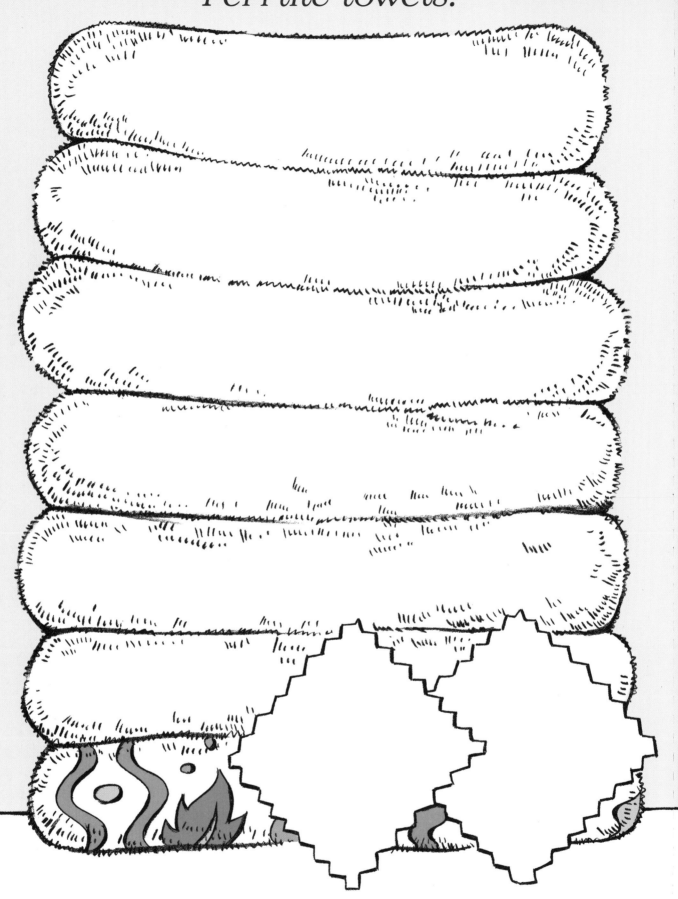

Create two contrasting designs for the towels.
Then complete the fluffy pile with your patterns.

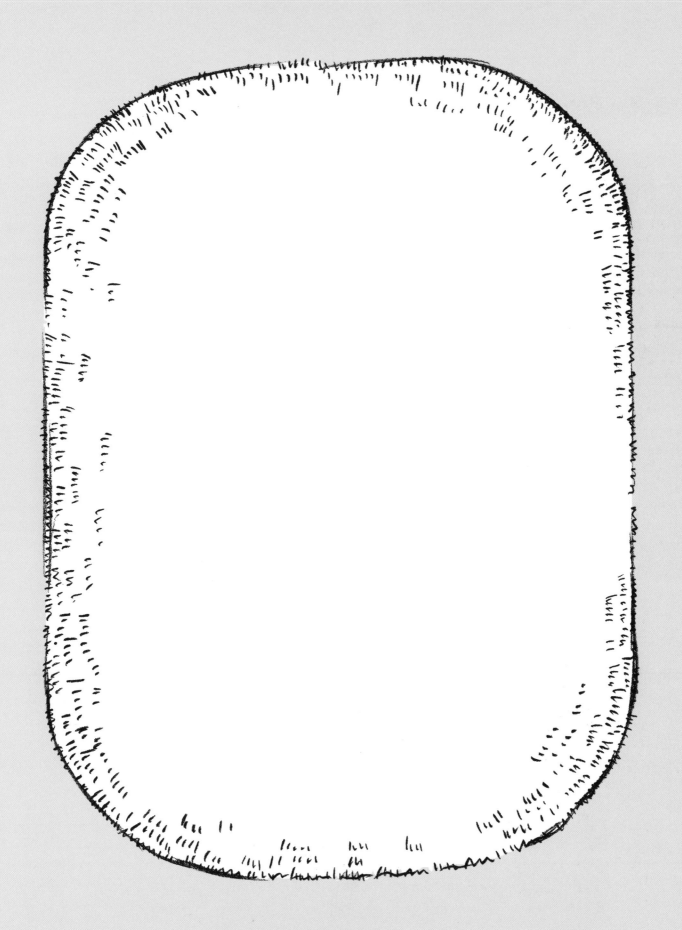

Now make this bath mat match.

Bathroom beauty zone.

Shed some light on your beauty with bulbs around the mirror.
Why not pop your own reflection in the frame?

The
Dining
Collection

Two for tea.

Design a pattern for the tea set on this cup and saucer.

Create a cloth for the table.

Now finish the tea set on the opposite page and put it on your newly designed tablecloth.

Doily delights.

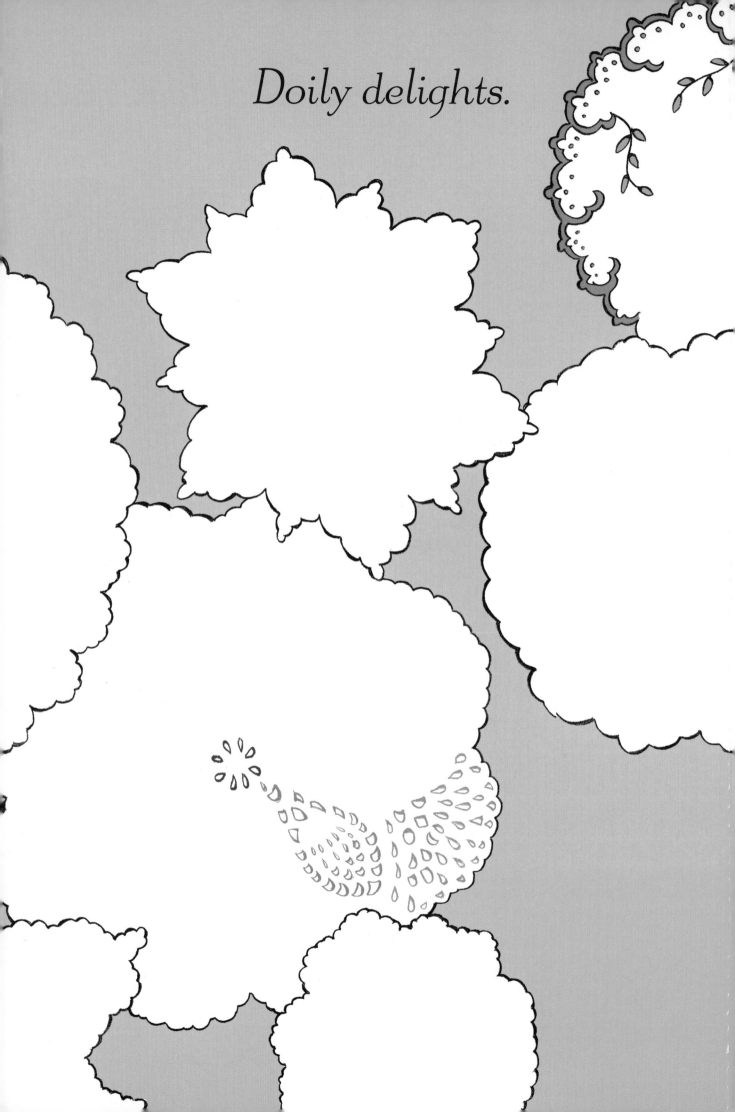

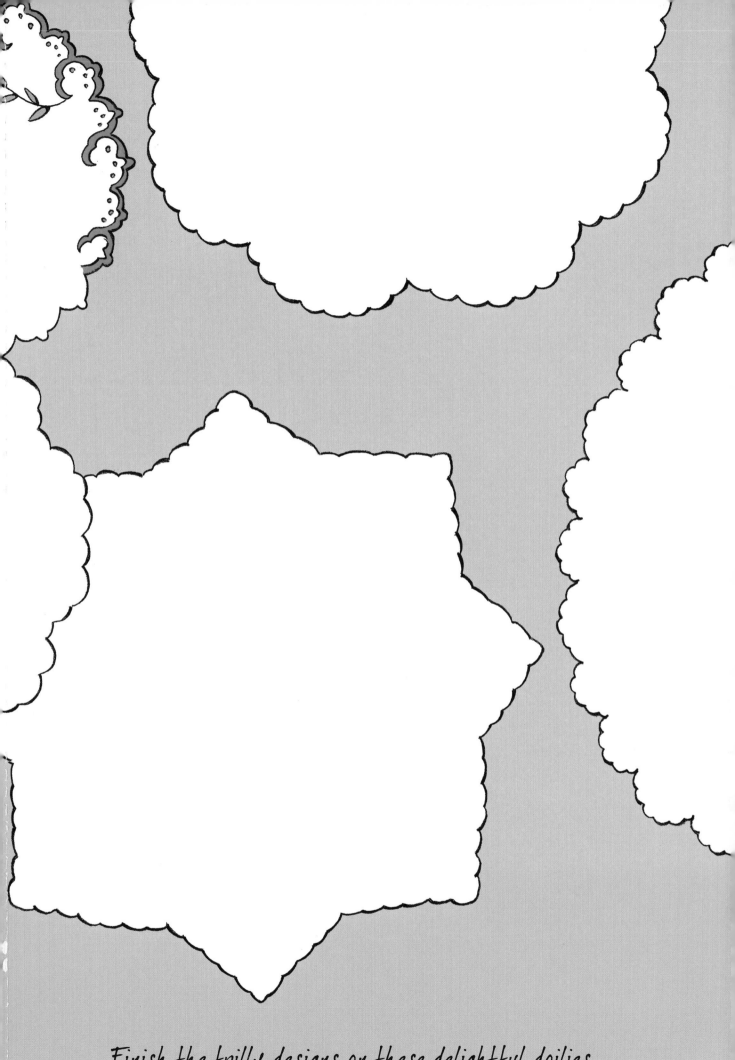

Finish the frilly designs on these delightful doilies.

Table touches to talk about.

Design some supercool cutlery and a stylish pattern for the plate.

Finish the floral centrepiece and decorate a place card.
Why not write your own name on it?

Serve up some serious style.

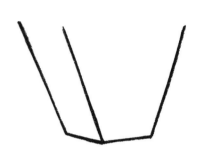

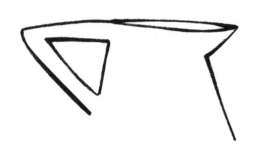

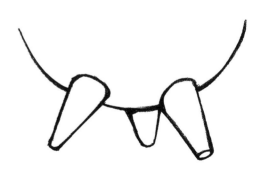

Fine food deserves fine china.
Finish the jugs, pots, and bowls.

Mix modern styles with vintage for that chic, thrown-together look.

Crystal clear.

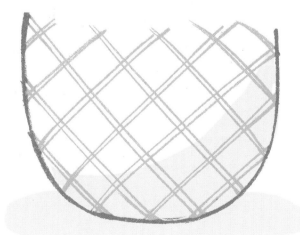

Ditch jugs and give these decanters the wow factor.

Sip in style.

Glamorous goblets are the new must-have glasses.

Make these goblets gorgeous.

Cherish your chairs.

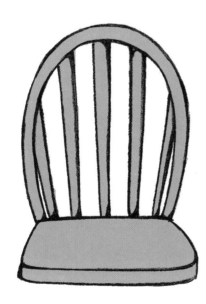

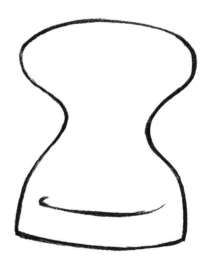

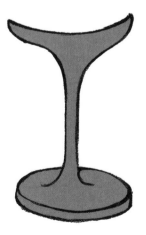

Finish the chairs with legs, backs, and pretty upholstery.

Plate date.

Cover the plates with
pretty patterns.

The gorgeous glow of candles.

Complete the candelabra.

Add more candles and glittering crystals to the chandelier.

Napkin time.

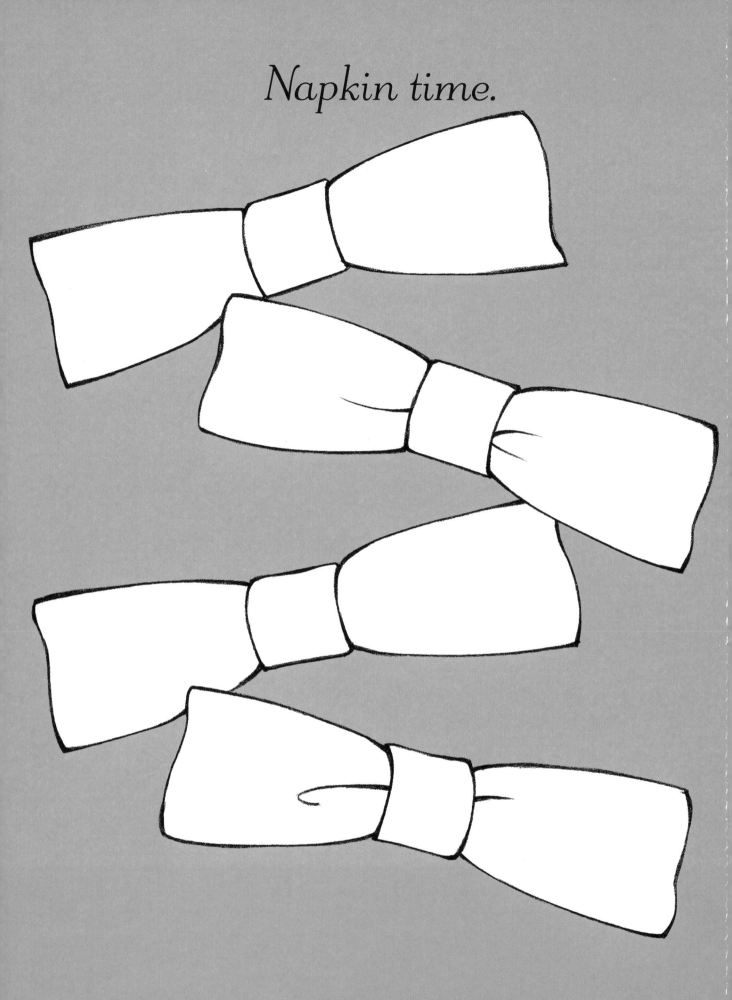

Decorate them, tuck them in, and
tuck into dinner with fabulous napkins.

A tempting tablecloth.

Design lovely linens to drape over your table.

Dresser to impress.

Give old dressers a stunning finish with antique handles.

The Bedroom Collection

Florals are big news in bedrooms.

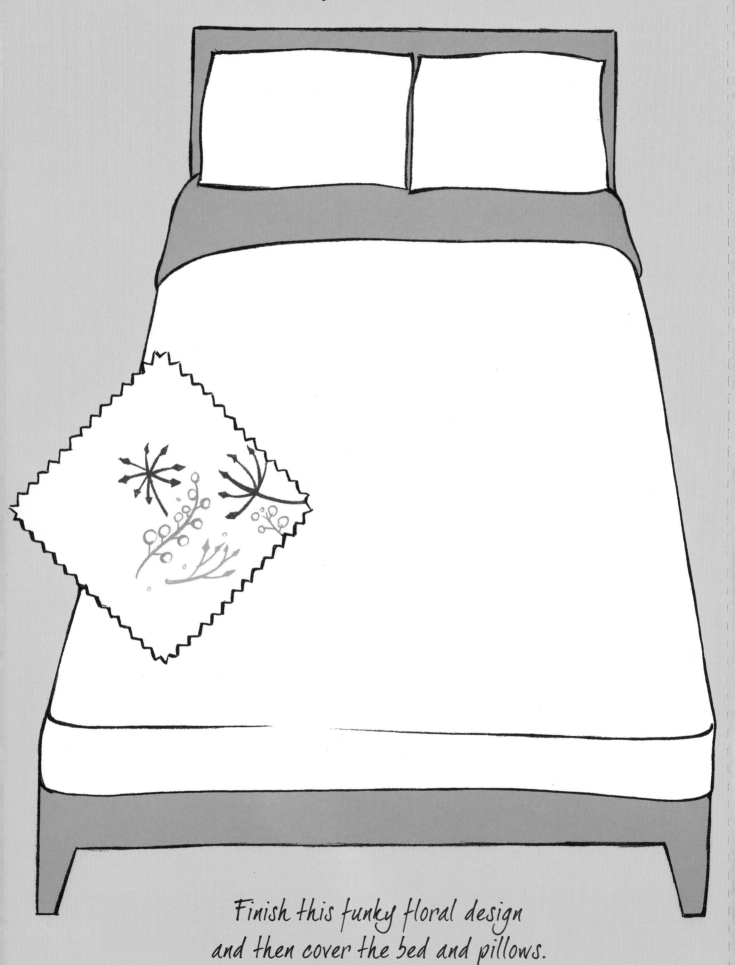

Finish this funky floral design
and then cover the bed and pillows.

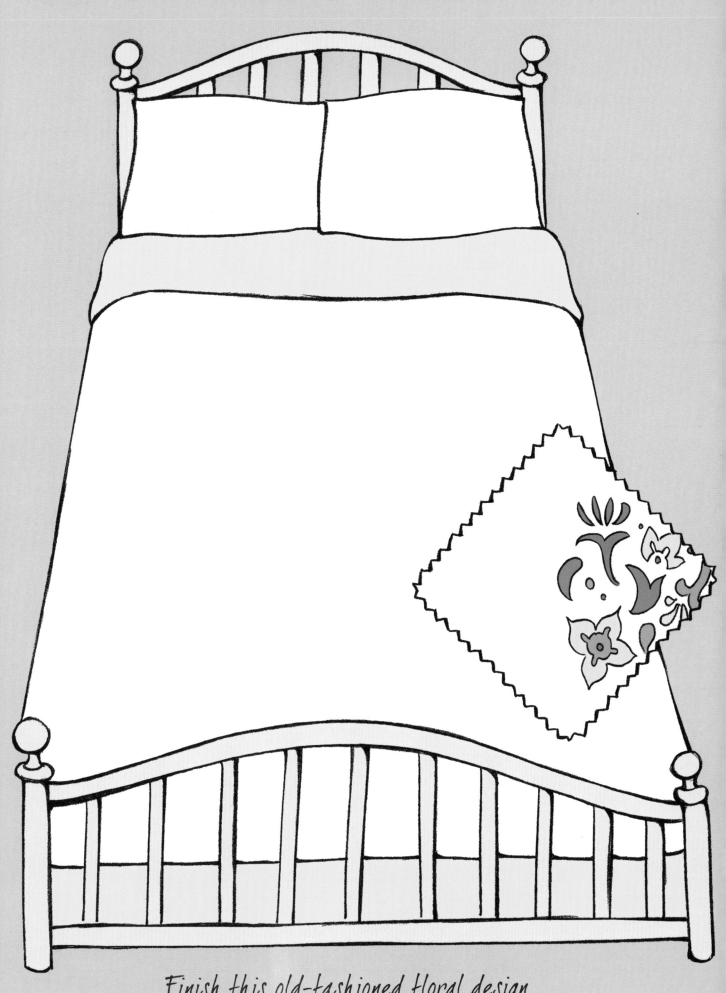

Finish this old-fashioned floral design
and then cover the bed and pillows.

Don't get hung up on furniture.

Finish the bedroom suite with doors and drawers.

Design a beautiful handle,
then add some to the
wardrobe and drawers.

Throw it on.

Throws can warm up any room.
Design the perfect pattern for a chilly night.

Bundle of joy.

Make this basket beautiful for a new baby.

A grown-up guest room.

Brighten up this plain guest room with eye-catching wallpaper, bold curtains, and beautiful bedding.

In with the new and the old.

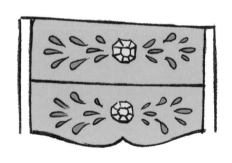

Vintage and modern, give these bedside tables tops or legs.

It's curtains for you!

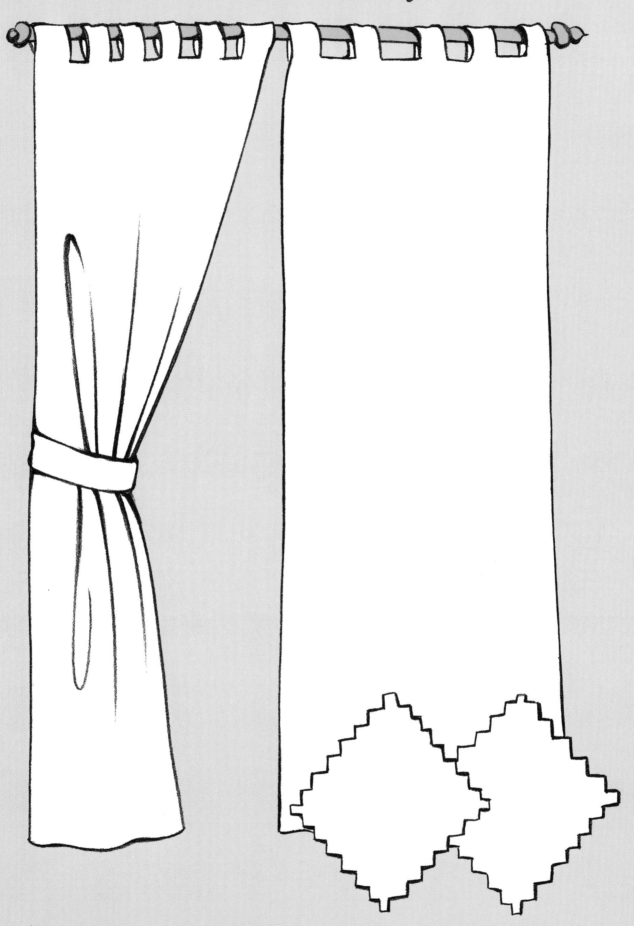

Design the fabric swatches and finish drapes to die for.

A night under a canopy.

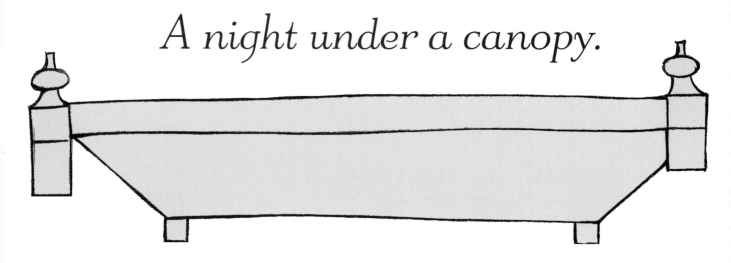

Finish the posts on this fabulous four-poster.

Pillows aplenty.

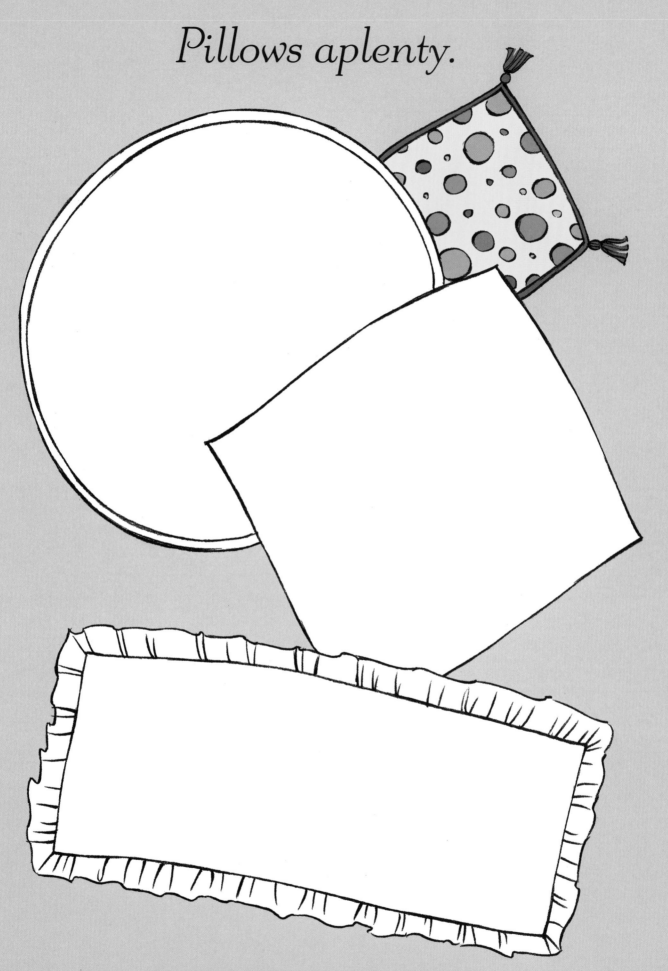

Pile the pillows and cushions high,
but give them some funky flair first.

A reflection on style.

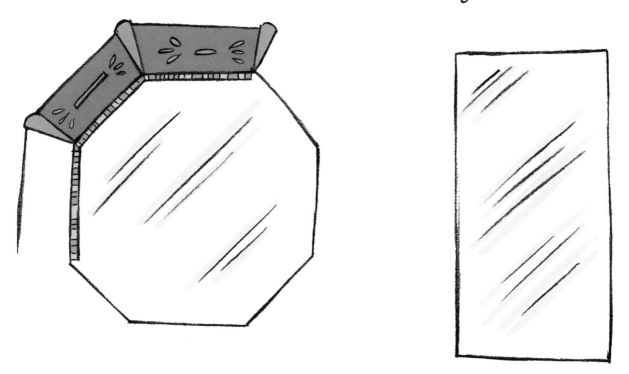

Mirrors can make a space look bigger by reflecting light into the room.

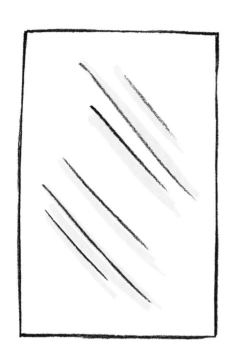

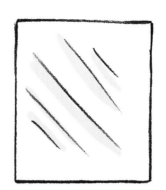

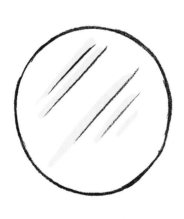

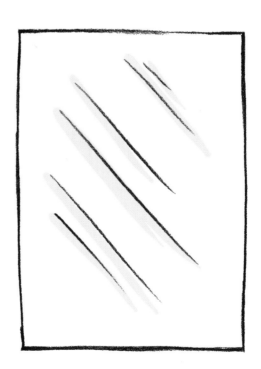

Give these mirrors marvelous frames.

The sweetest dreams.

Finish the fresco on the ceiling.

The Kitchen Collection

Kitchen style.

Decorate the cupboards and fill the hooks with
your own range of pans.

Fridge magnetism.

Cover the fridge with bright and funky magnets.

Purrr-fect!

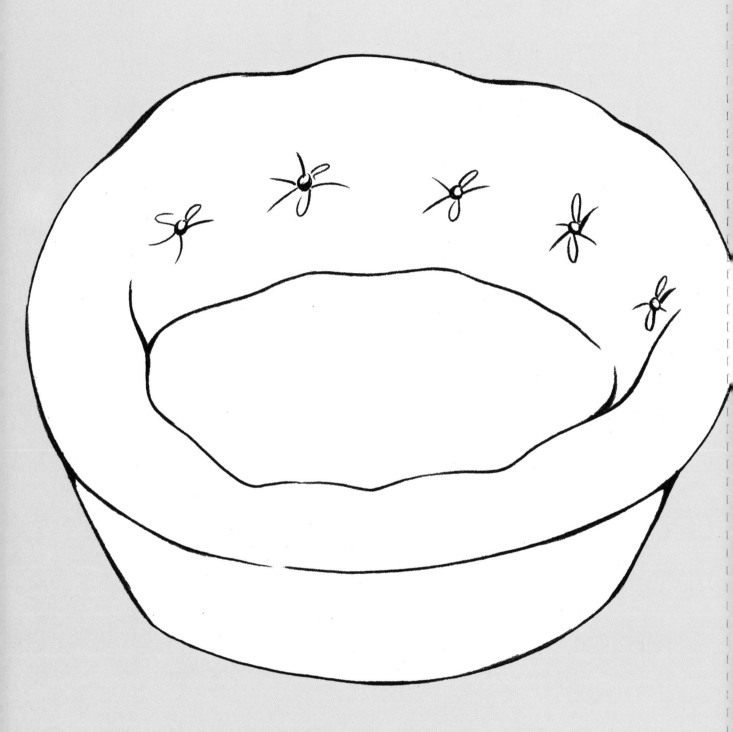

Give your feline friends a stylish bed to lounge in.

Delish dish.

Design a pet-friendly pattern for this bowl.

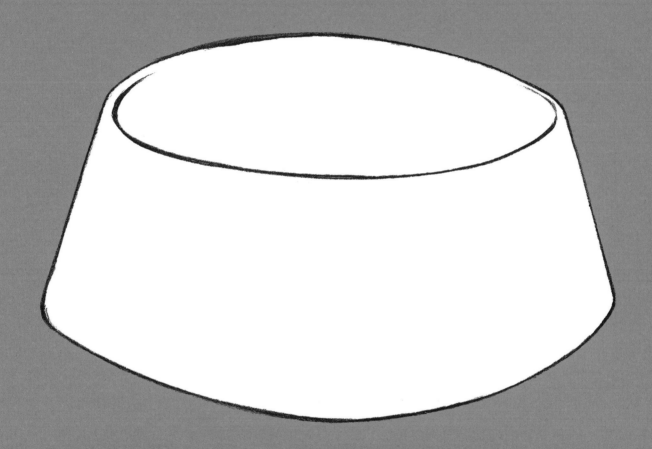

Let your pooch eat in style.
Design a pet-friendly pattern for this bowl.

Toast of the town.

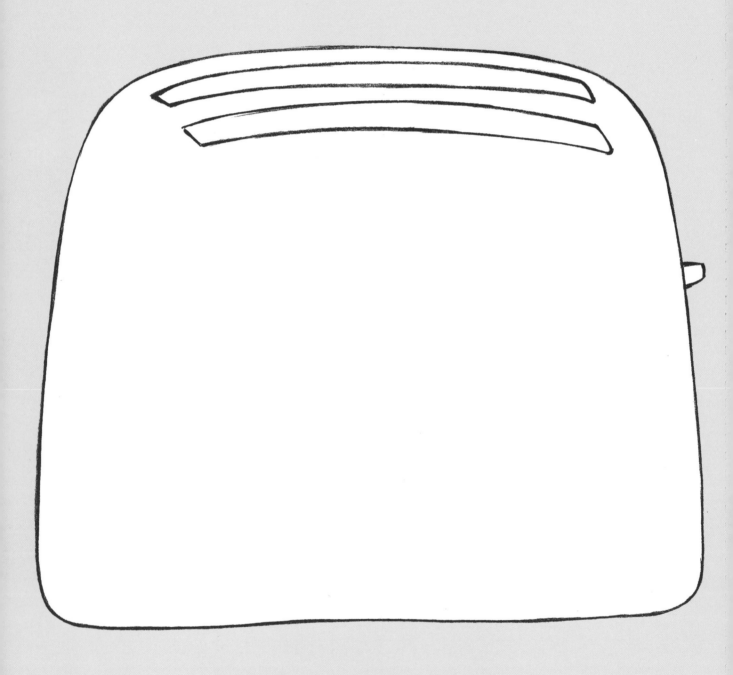

Create a bold design for the toaster . . .

Put the kettle on trend.

. . . and one for the kettle.

The sweet life.

Get a candy-shop look by filling jars
with colorful sweet treats.

Funky, fruity features.

Create a super centerpiece with a fully stocked fruit bowl.

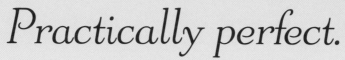

Practically perfect.

Design a stylish set of tea towels
for mopping up spills.

Tune in to great style.

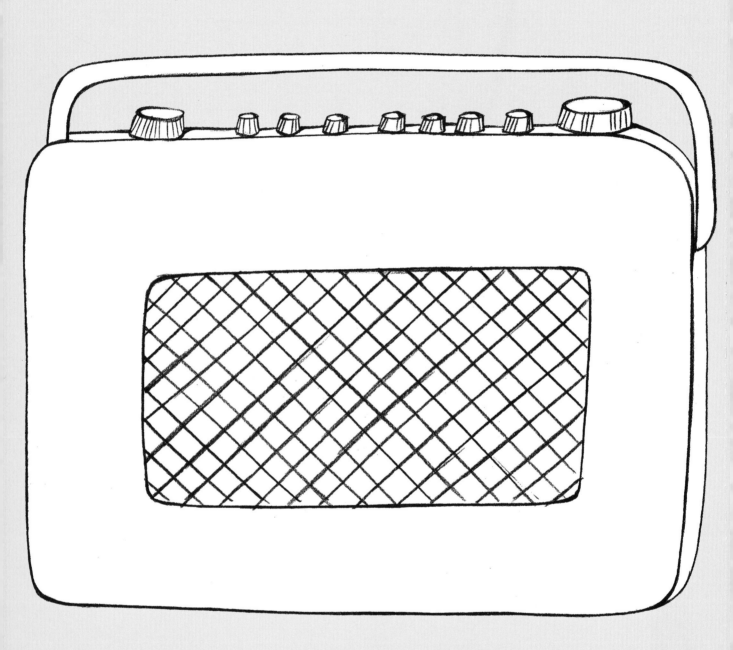

Give this radio a groovy design
for some toe-tapping tunes to cook by.

Keep everything at hand.

Draw a jaw-dropping jar to store utensils.

Captivating canisters.

Decorate these handy storage jars.

Make sure you label what's in them!

Styled high.

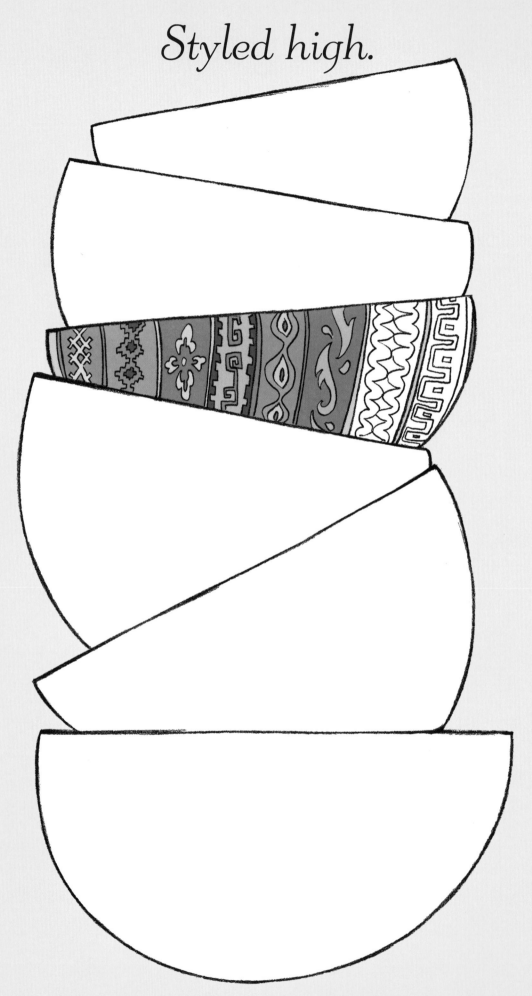

Use your noodle to decorate these soup bowls.

Finishing Touches

Fantastic feature wallpapers.

Finish the out-of-this-world design.

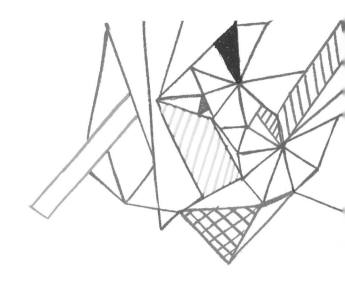

Finish the modern, geometric design on this wallpaper.

Add floral features to bring the outdoors indoors
with this fabulous wallpaper.

Heaven is homemade.

Finish the cushion with prettily patterned patches.

Look on the bright side.

Give these lampshades illuminating designs.

In the frame.

Flamboyant frames add flair to pictures.

Can you create frames that match the pictures inside them?

But is it art?

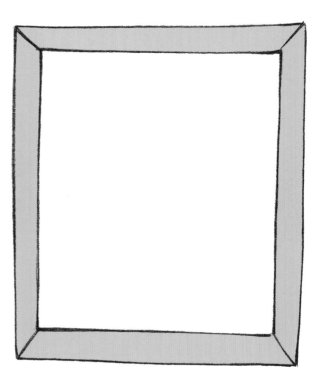

*Fill these frames and stands
with fantastic pieces of modern art.*

Glowing glamour.

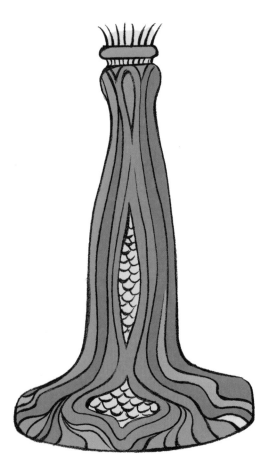

Finish this classic lamp with a dainty design.

Light up the room by decorating
this charming Chinese lantern.

Not-so-standard lamps.

Create pools of flattering light with beautiful lampshades.

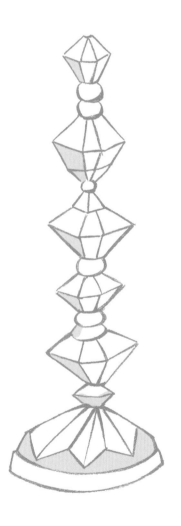

Finish their stands and shades.

Passionate about pottery.

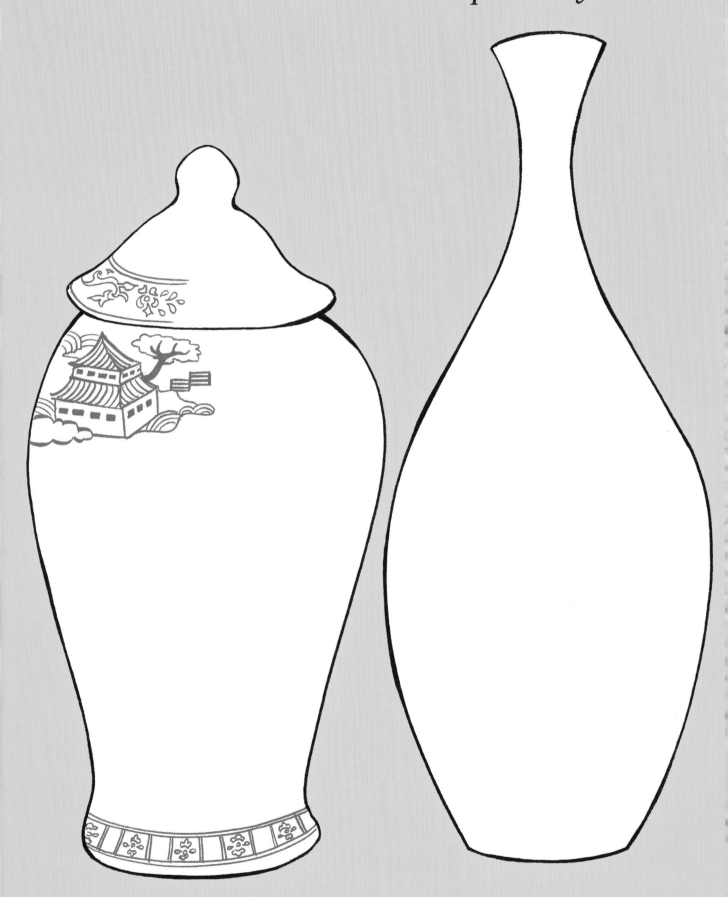

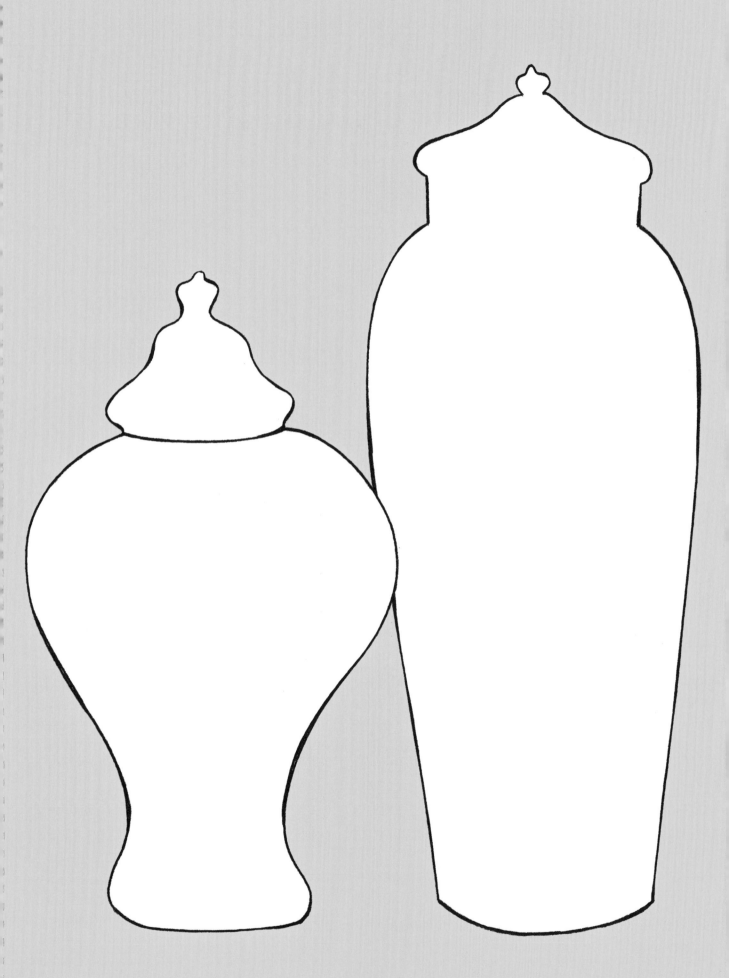

Give these Japanese-style jars and vases beautiful designs.

That's so bazaar!

Give your room an exotic twist with
Moroccan lighting.
Finish these fabulous lamps.

Move with the times.

A cool clock adds a bold statement to any wall.

Give these clocks funky frames.

Take a walk on the wild side!

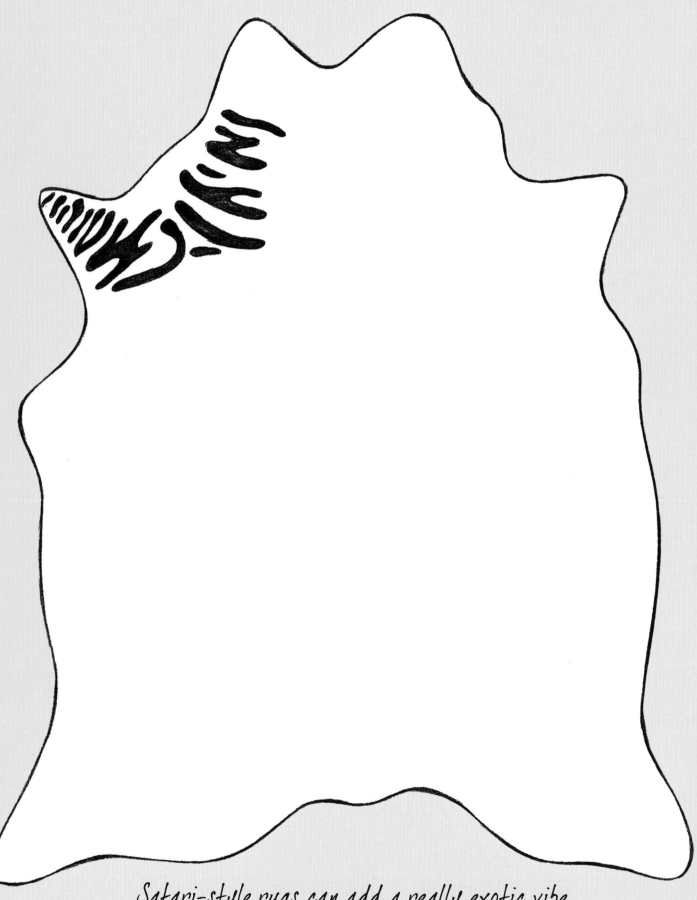

Safari-style rugs can add a really exotic vibe.
Finish the zebra pattern on this fake-fur rug.

Let's get tribal.

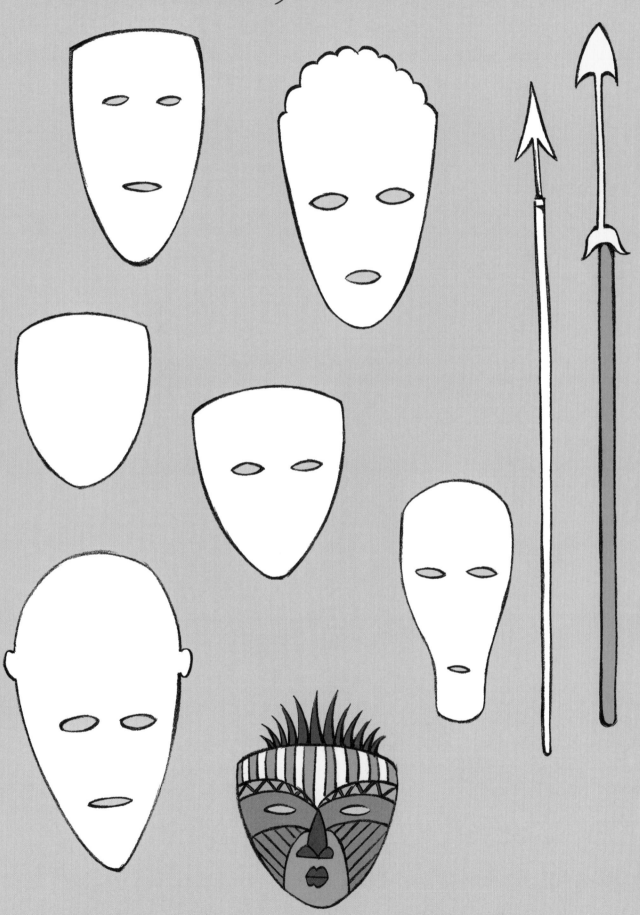

Finish these masks to add an African feel.

Superb storage solutions.

Make these storage boxes beautiful.

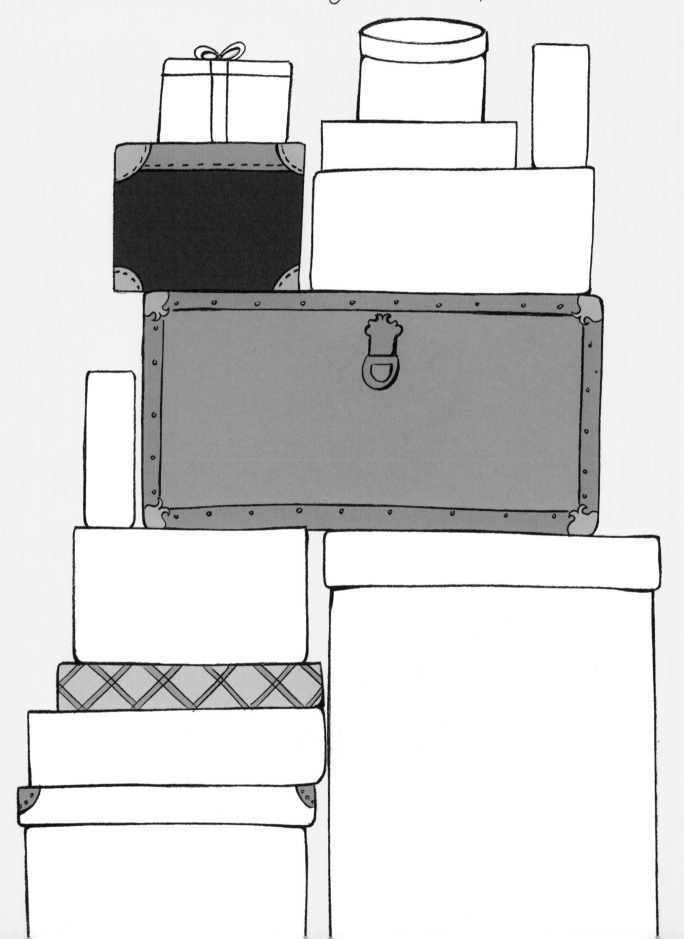

Screen dream.

Screens add shape to a room.
Finish the design to create a cool, calm space.

Branch out into bonsai.

Miniature trees make a fresh statement.
Finish the branches on this bonsai.

The Garden Collection

Throw open the patio doors.

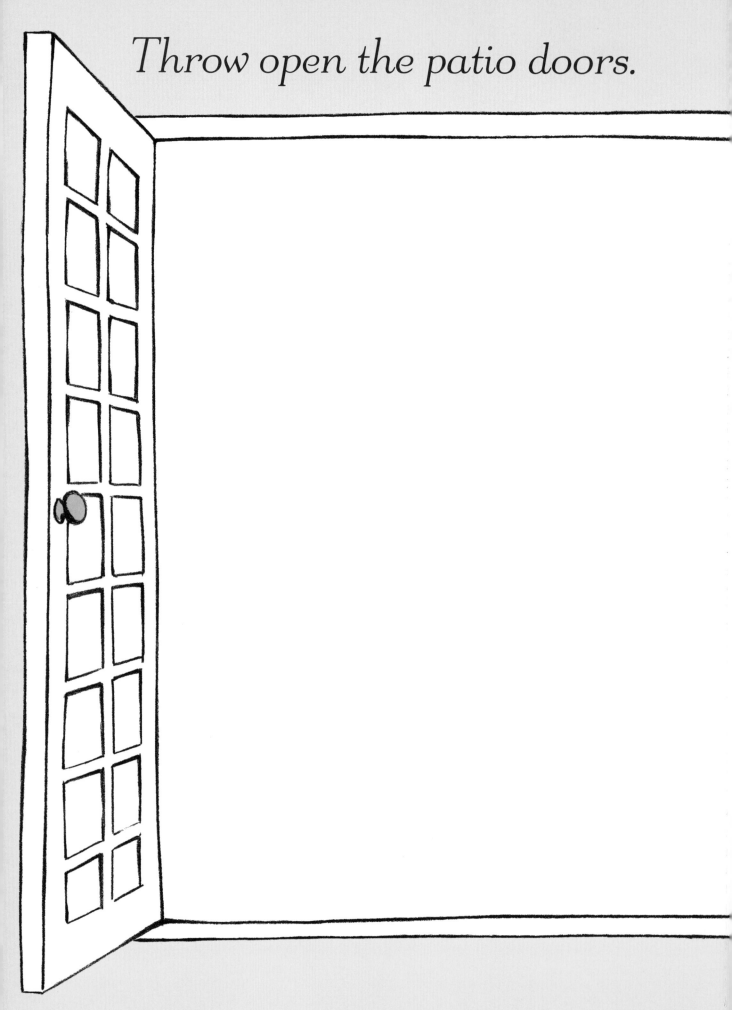

A gorgeous garden view is a great addition to any room.

Draw a beautiful garden.

First impressions . . .

Gorgeous gates add grandeur to any driveway.
Finish the iron gates.

. . . that last a lifetime.

Design a divine door knocker and mailbox for this door and add a number to show which house it is.

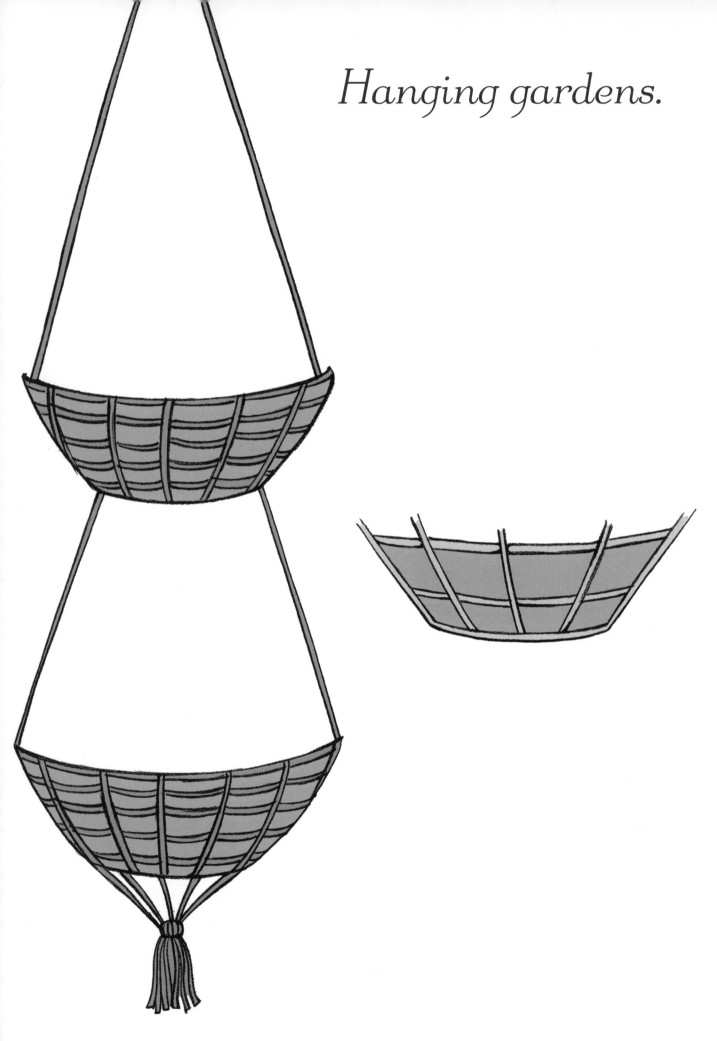

Hanging gardens.

Bold baskets brighten up even the smallest outside spaces.

Fill the hanging baskets with beautiful flowers and foliage.

Top topiary tubs.

Shaped bushes and small trees can add a dramatic look.

Fill the planters with shaped bushes and trees.

A midsummer night's dream.

Create a magical fairyland for a delightful outdoor dinner.

Get in the swing.

There's nothing like a hammock for chilling out.

Finish the fabulous fringe on this luxurious hammock.

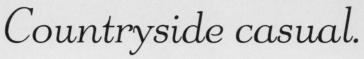

Countryside casual.

Finish the cute cottage and fill the garden with flowers.

Splash out.

Finish the fountain to create a tranquil outside space.

Camping out.

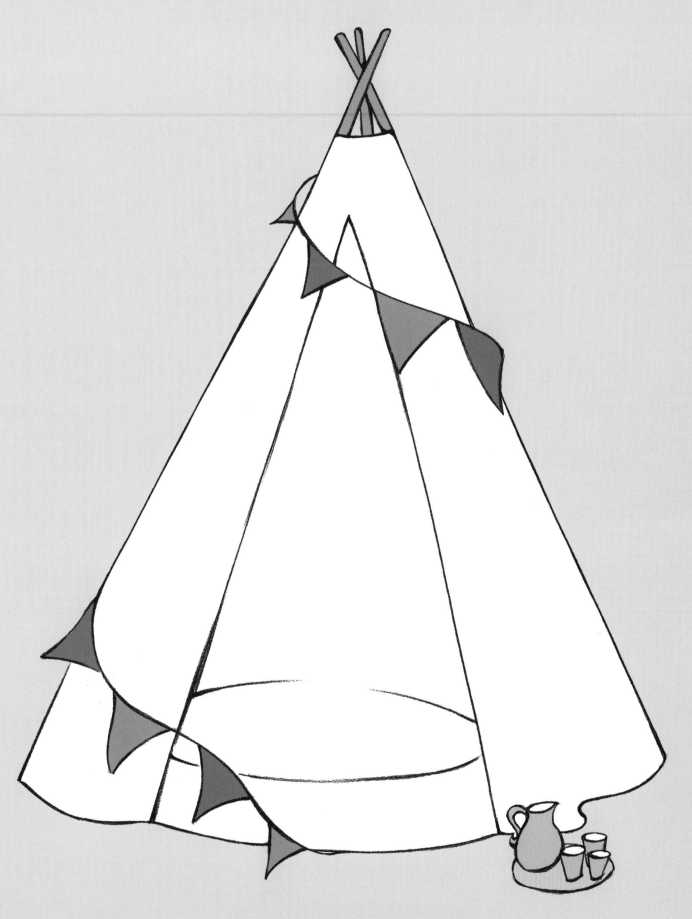

Decorate the teepee tent for a midnight campout.

Sit back and relax.

*Design a fabric
for the pillow . . .*

*Fabrics aren't just for the interior.
Brighten up this outdoor cushion with bold prints.*

Cover the lounge in the fabric
you designed.

. . . and one for
the lounge.

Flowers, flowers everywhere.

Add fresh flowers to these window boxes.

Stellar statues.

Statues add a personal touch to any garden.
Finish these stupendous statues.

It's cool in the shade.

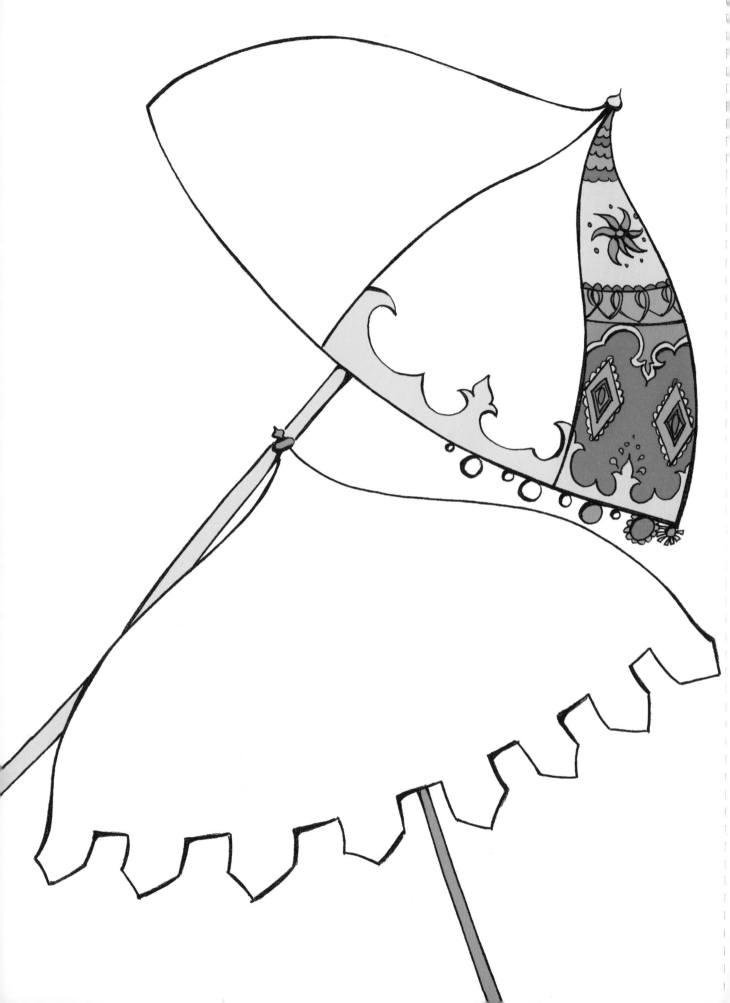

Stay out of the sun in style. Decorate these pretty parasols.

In the doghouse.

People aren't the only ones who need a stylish place to sleep.
Give this kennel a fabulous makeover.

The
Interior Design
Studio

The good-mood board.

Inspiration can strike at any time.

Fill the board with pictures and pieces of fabric.

Your very own design studio.

Fill the shelves with beautiful things to inspire your designs.

Window shopping.

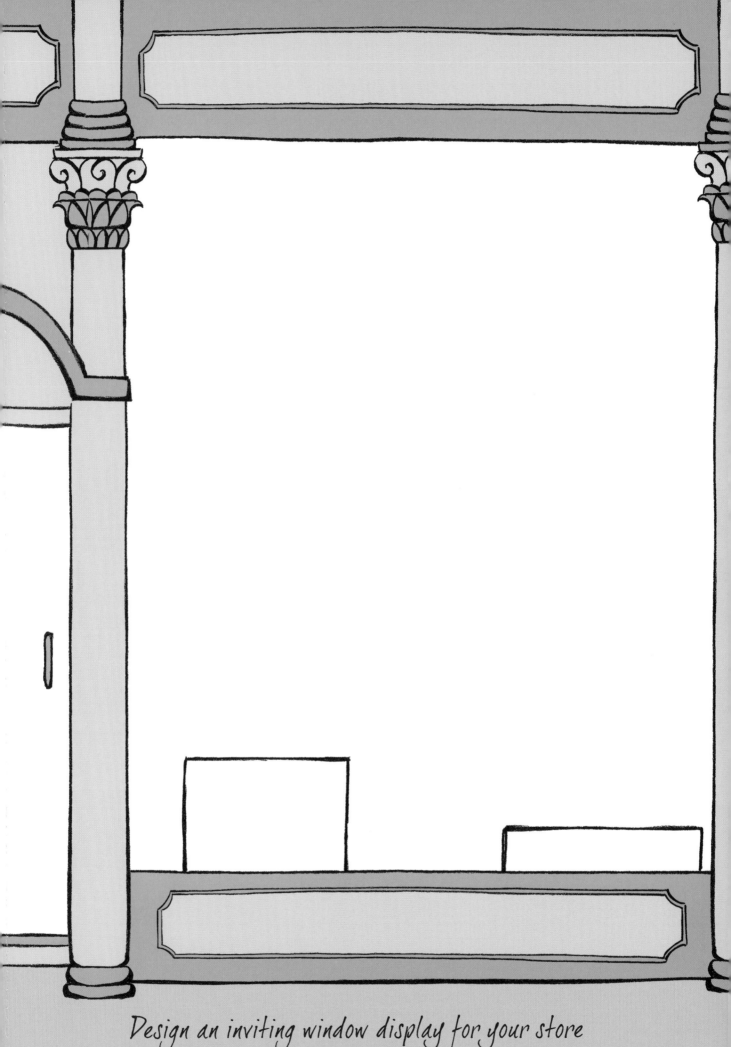

Design an inviting window display for your store
to get the customers flocking in.

It's not a catalog; it's a lifestyle.

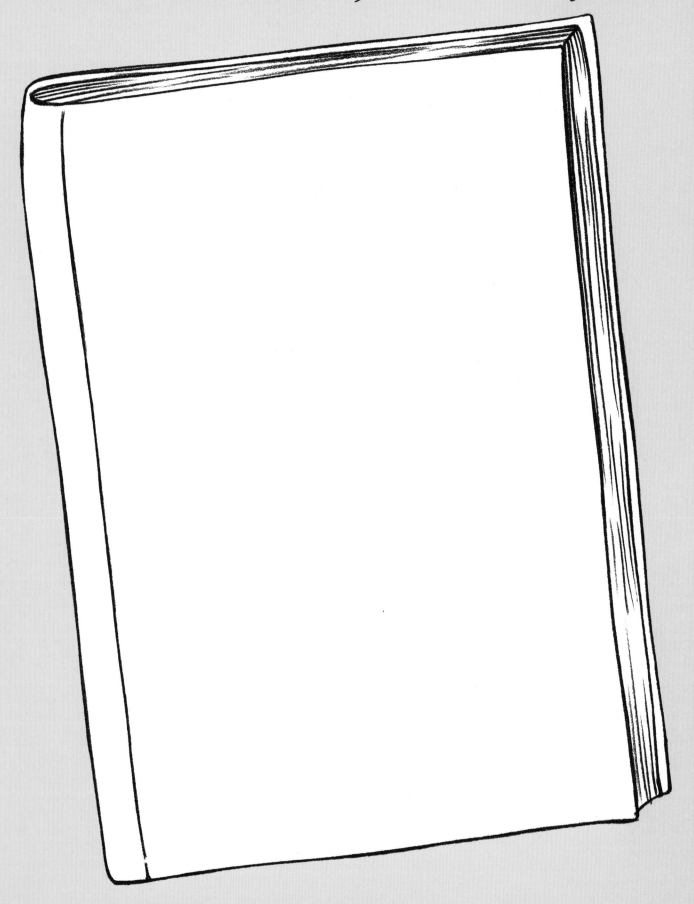

Design a beautiful catalog to show off your divine designs.

Get carried away.

Cool paper bags will advertise your store far and wide.
Give your bags a bold design.

On the shop floor.

Arrange items in your store. What price are they?